FastTrack™
MUSIC INSTRUCTION

Bass 1

INTRODUCTION

Welcome back to FastTrack™!

Hope you enjoyed Bass 1 and are ready to play some hits. Have you and your friends formed a band? Or do you feel like soloing with the audio tracks? Either way, make sure you're turned up loud...it's time to jam!

With the knowledge you already have, you're ready to play all of these eight songs. But it's still important to remember the three Ps: **patience**, **practice** and **pace yourself**.

As with Bass 1, don't try to bite off more than you can chew. If your fingers hurt, take some time off. If you get frustrated, put down your bass, relax and just listen to the track. If you forget a note position or rhythmic value, go back and learn it. If you're doing fine, think about charging admission.

CONTENTS

ABOUT THE AUDIO

Again, you get audio tracks with the book! Each song in the book is included, so you can hear how it sounds and play along when you're ready.

Each audio example is preceded by one measure of "clicks" to indicate the tempo and meter. Pan right to hear the bass part emphasized. Pan left to hear the accompaniment emphasized.

PLAYBACK+
Speed • Pitch • Balance • Loop

To access audio visit:
www.halleonard.com/mylibrary

Enter Code
3521-8194-2322-5140

HAL•LEONARD®
CORPORATION
7777 W. BLUEMOUND RD. P.O. BOX 13819 MILWAUKEE, WI 53213

Visit Hal Leonard online at
www.halleonard.com

T0052805

LEARN SOMETHING NEW EACH DAY

We know you're eager to play, but first you need to learn a few new things. We'll make it brief—only two pages...

Melody and Lyrics

All of the melody lines and lyrics to these great songs (except for "Walk Don't Run" which is an instrumental) are included for your musical pleasure (and benefit). These are shown on an extra musical staff, which we added above your part.

Unfortunately, bass players never (OK, rarely) play the melody, but this added vocal line will help you follow the song more easily as you play your part.

And whether you have a singer in the band or decide to carry the tune yourself, this new staff is your key to adding some vocals to your tunes.

Endings

Several of the songs have some interesting little symbols that you must understand before playing. Each of these symbols represents a different type of **ending**.

1st, 2nd, and 3rd Endings

You know two of these from *Bass 1* (the brackets with numbers 1 and 2):

REMINDER: Simply play the song through to the first ending, repeat back to the first repeat sign, or beginning of the song (whichever is the case). Play through the song again, but skip the first ending and play the second ending.

Two songs, "Gimme Some Lovin'" and "Jailhouse Rock," have a **3rd ending**.

But this is really nothing really new (just a bracket with a number 3). It's the same principle as a 2nd ending—just one more repeat and ending for one more terrific melody.

D.S. al Coda

When you see these words, go back and repeat from this symbol: 𝄋

Play until you see the words *"to Coda"* then skip to the Coda, indicated by this symbol: 𝄌

Now just finish the song.

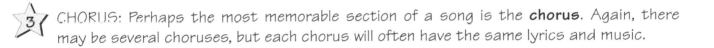

Song Structure

Most songs have different sections, which might be recognizable by any or all of the following:

 INTRODUCTION (or "intro"): This is a short section at the beginning that (you guessed it again!) "introduces" the song to the listeners.

2 VERSES: One of the main sections of the song is the **verse**. There will usually be several verses, all with the same music but each with different lyrics.

3 CHORUS: Perhaps the most memorable section of a song is the **chorus**. Again, there may be several choruses, but each chorus will often have the same lyrics and music.

4 BRIDGE: This section makes a transition from one part of a song to the next. For example, you may find a bridge between the chorus and next verse.

 SOLOS: Sometimes solos are played over the verse or chorus structure, but in some songs the solo section has its own structure. This is your time to stand back and show your support for the soloist.

6 OUTRO: Similar to the "intro," this section brings the song to an end.

That's about it! Enjoy the music...

Evil Ways

Words and Music by Sonny Henry

A Intro

Moderate Latin ♩ = 122

1. You got to change your e - vil

B Verse

ways, ba - by, be - fore I start
2.,3. home, ba - by, my house is dark and my

To Coda ⊕

lov - in' you. You got to change, ___ ba - by,
thoughts are cold. You hang a - round, ___ ba - by,

and ev -'ry word ___ that I say is true. You got me run - nin' and hid - in' all ___
with Gene and Joan ___ and a who knows who. I'm get - tin' tired ___ of wait - in' and

___ o - ver town. ___ You got me sneak - in' and a-peep - in' and run - nin' me down. ___ This can't go
fool - in' a - round. ___ I'll find some - bod - y that ___ won't make me feel like a clown. ___ This can't go

on. }
on. }
Lord ___ knows you got to change, ba -

- by,   baby.   When I come

change.

C Organ Solo

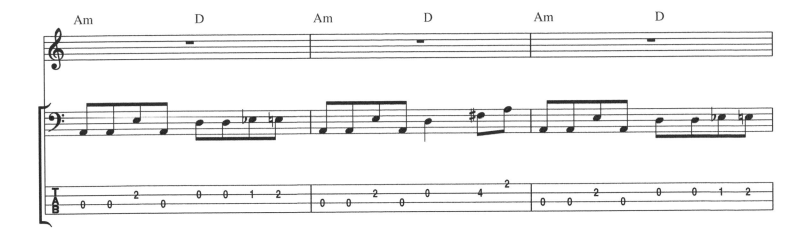

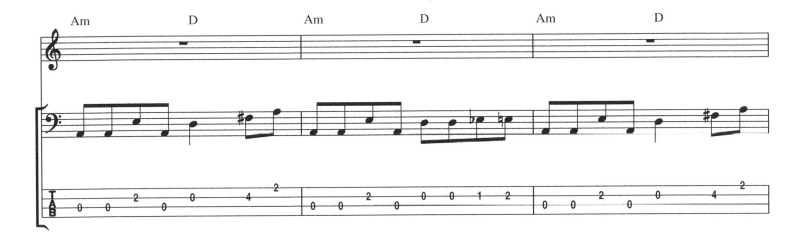

D.S. al Coda

When I come

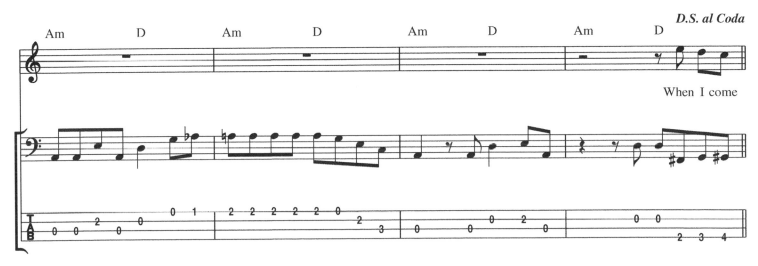

Gimme Some Lovin'

Words and Music by Spencer Davis, Muff Winwood and Steve Winwood

A Intro

Moderately Fast ♩ = 152

B Interlude

G

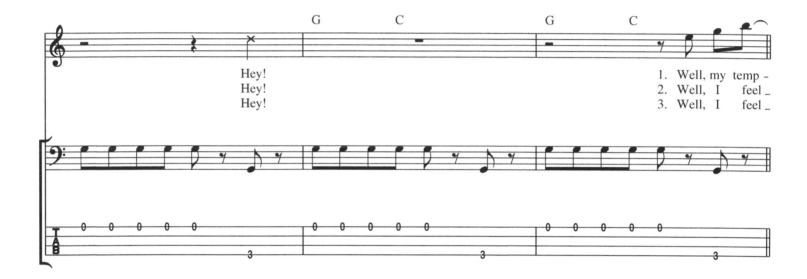

Hey!
Hey!
Hey!

1. Well, my temp -
2. Well, I feel _
3. Well, I feel _

C Verse

- 'ra-ture's ris-ing as my feet hit the floor. _   Cra-zy peo-ple knock-in' just a-
   so good. ___ Ev-'ry-thing is kind-a high.   You bet-ter take it ea-sy 'cause the
   so good. ___ Ev-'ry-thing is kind-a high.   You bet-ter take it ea-sy 'cause the

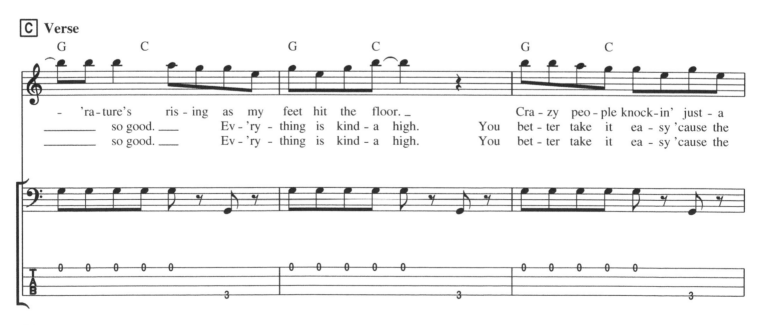

(Gim-me gim-me some lov - in'.) Gim-me some _ a lov-in'. Ev - 'ry day. _

1., 2.

3.

(Gim-me, gim-me some lov - in'.)

(Gim-me, gim-me some lov - in'.)

Gloria

Words and Music by Van Morrison

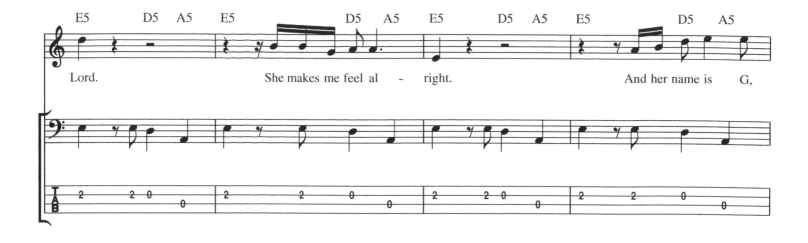

Lord.   She makes me feel al - right.   And her name is   G,

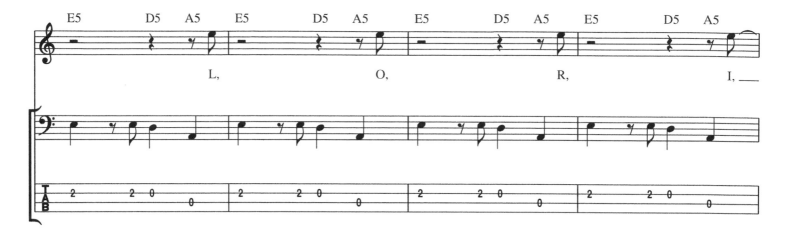

L,   O,   R,   I, ___

%

C Chorus

___ I I I,   G L O R I A.   (Glo - ri - a.)   G-L-O-R-I-A.

(Glo - ri - a.)   I'm gon-na shout it all ___ night,   (Glo - ri - a.)   I'm gon-na shout it ev-'ry day.

14

Yeah yeah — yeah yeah yeah yeah yeah.
(Glo - ri - a.)

D **Interlude**

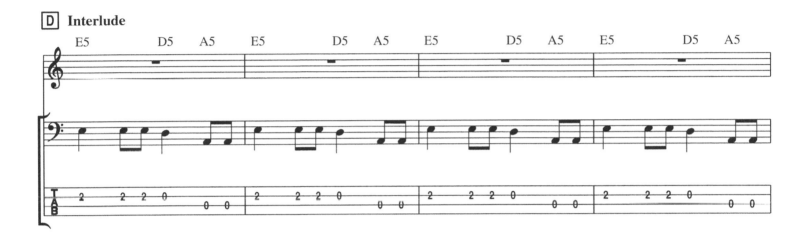

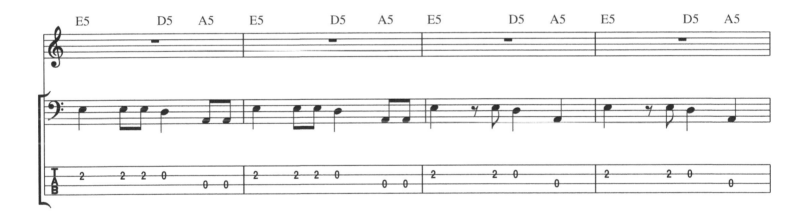

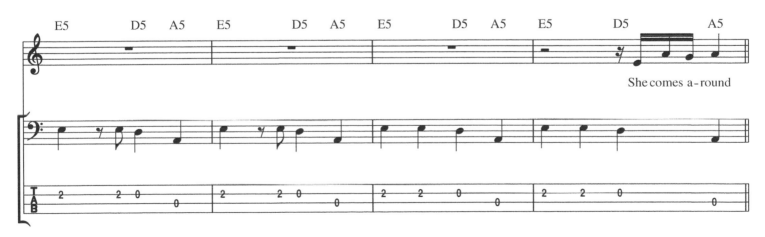

She comes a-round

Verse 2

⊕ *Coda*

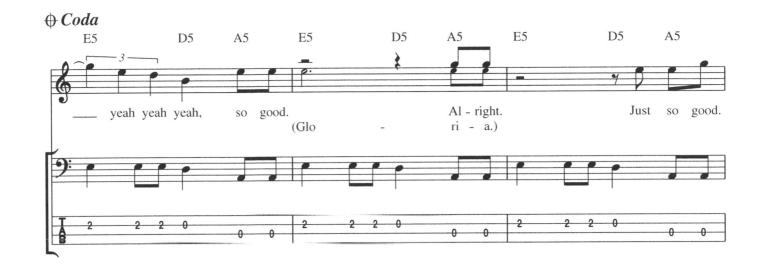

F Outro

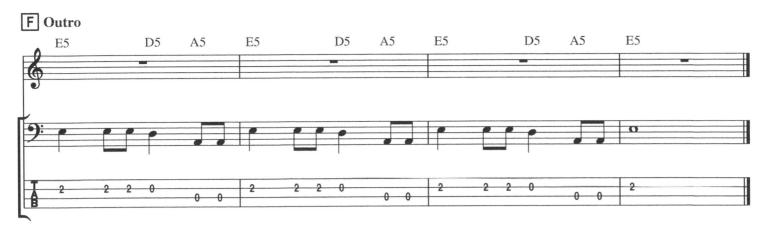

4 Have I Told You Lately

Words and Music by Van Morrison

A Intro

Stately ♩ = 74

B Chorus

Have I told you late-ly that I love you? Have I

told you there's no one else a-bove ___ you?

Fill my heart ___ with glad-ness,

take a-way all ___ my sad-ness, ease my trou-bles that's ___ what you do.

For the

we should give thanks and pray ___ to the one, _ to the one. _ Have I

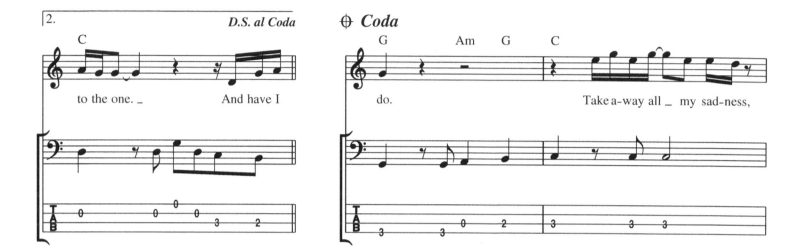

to the one. _ And have I

do. Take a-way all _ my sad-ness,

Fill my life with glad-ness, ease my trou-bles that's _ what you do.

Take a-way all _ my sad-ness, fill my heart with glad - ness, ease my trou-bles that's _ what you do. ___

rit.

Jailhouse Rock

Words and Music by Jerry Leiber and Mike Stoller

C **Chorus**

rock!   Ev - 'ry - bod — y, let's   rock!   Ev - 'ry - bod - y in the whole   cell   block   was danc -

|1., 2.| |3.|

To Coda ⊕

- ing   to   the   Jail - house   Rock!   Rock!

D **Guitar Solo**

Additional Lyrics

3. Number Forty-seven said to number Three:
   "You're the cutest jailbird I ever did see.
   I sure would be delighted with your company.
   Come on and do the Jailhouse Rock with me."

4. The sad sack was a-sittin' on a block of stone,
   Way over in a corner weeping all alone.
   The warden said: "Hey, Buddy, don't you be no square,
   If you can't find a partner, use a wooden chair!"

(optional)

5. Shifty Henry said to Bugs: "For heaven's sake.
   No one's lookin', now's our chance to make a break."
   Bugsy turned to Shifty and he said, "Nix, nix;
   I wanna stick around a while and get my kicks."

Time Is on My Side

Words and Music by Jerry Ragovoy

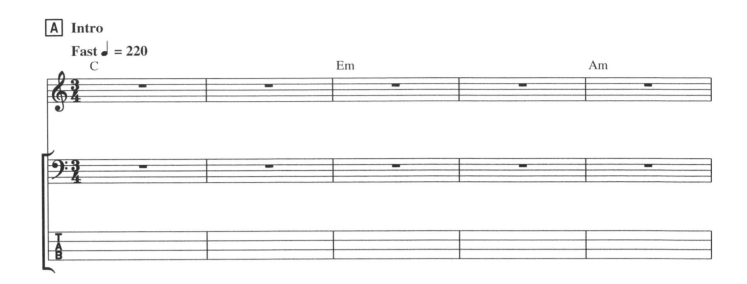

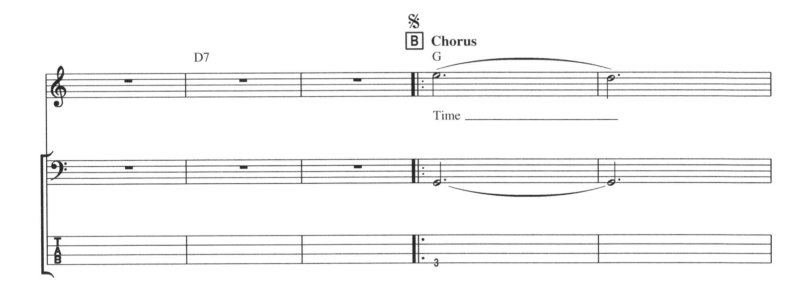

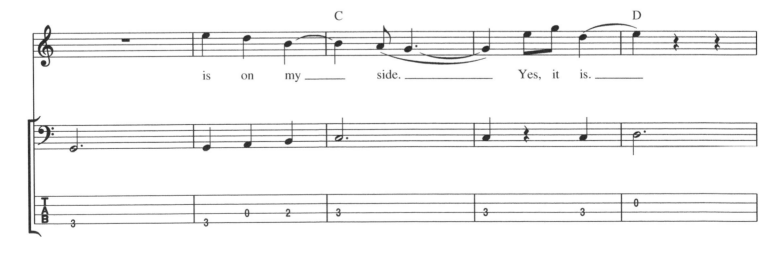

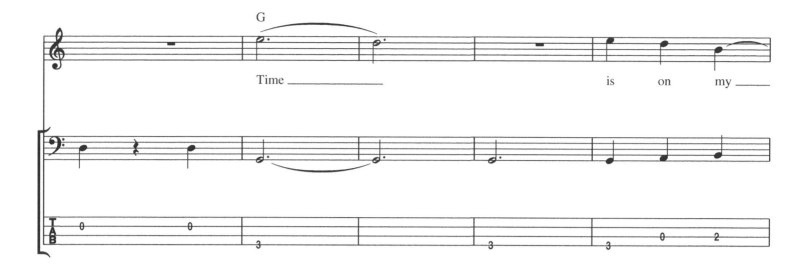

Time _____ is on my _____

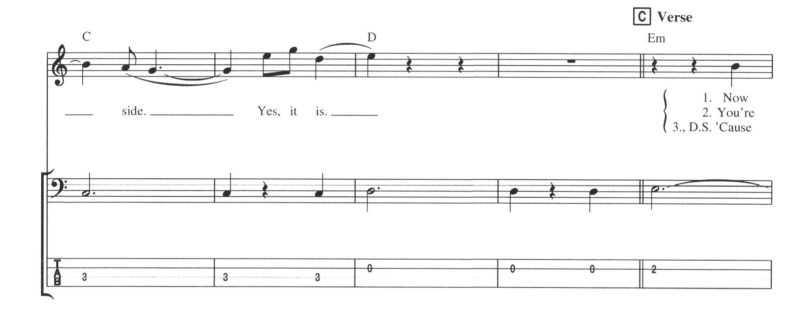

_____ side. _____ Yes, it is. _____

C Verse

1. Now
2. You're
3., D.S. 'Cause

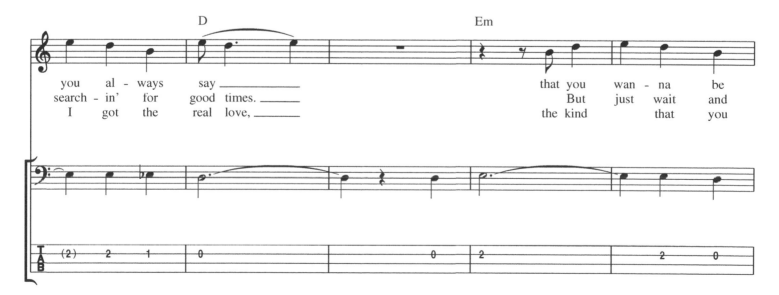

you al - ways say _____ that you wan - na be
search - in' for good times. _____ But just wait and
I got the real love, _____ the kind that you

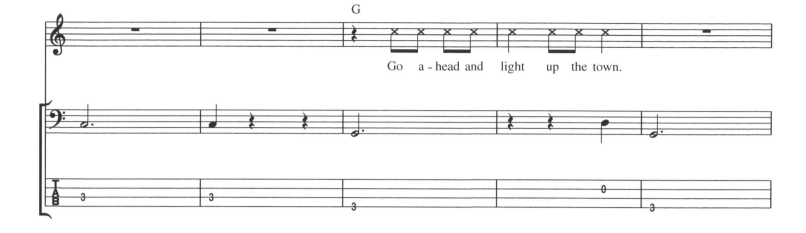

Go a-head and light up the town.

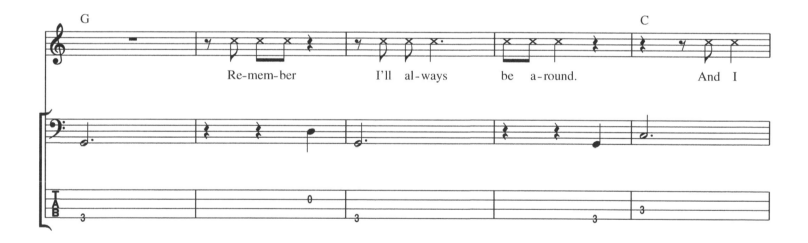

And, ba - by, do ev - 'ry-thing your heart de - sires.

Re-mem-ber I'll al-ways be a-round. And I

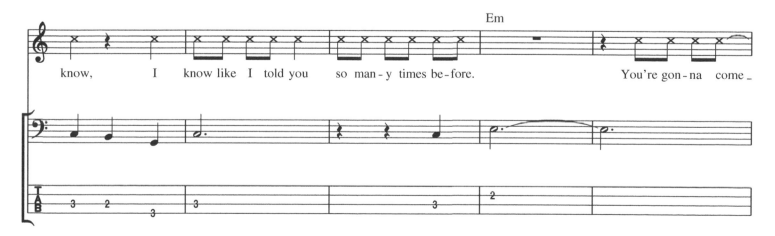

know, I know like I told you so man-y times be-fore. You're gon-na come

D.S. al Coda

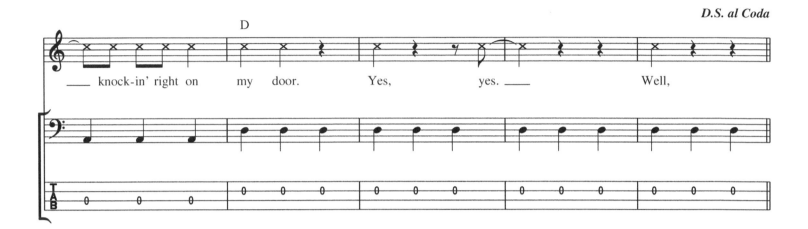

Twist and Shout

Words and Music by Bert Russell and Phil Medley

29

Walk Don't Run

Words and Music by Johnny Smith

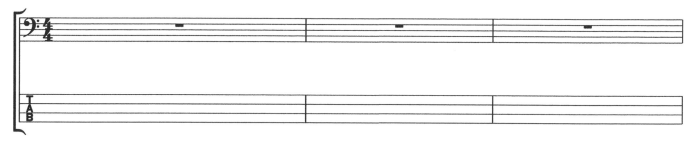

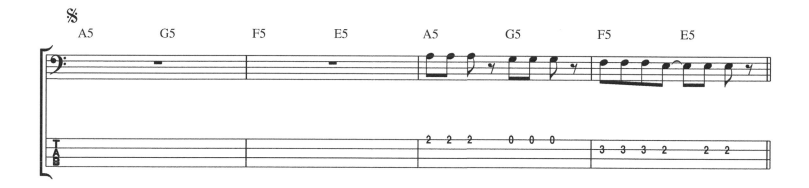

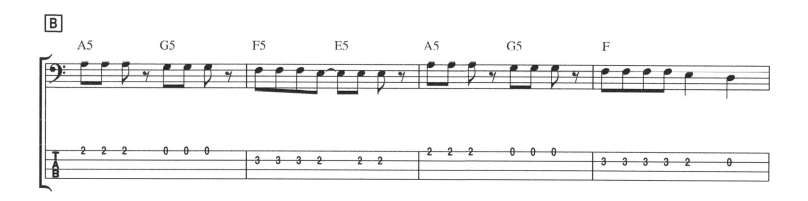

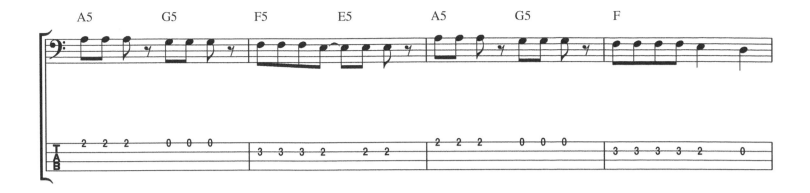

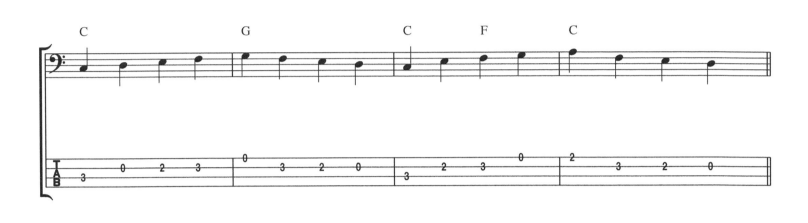

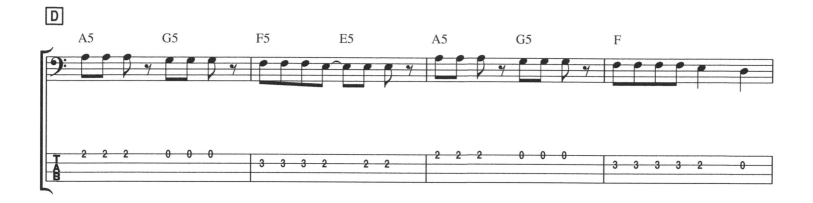

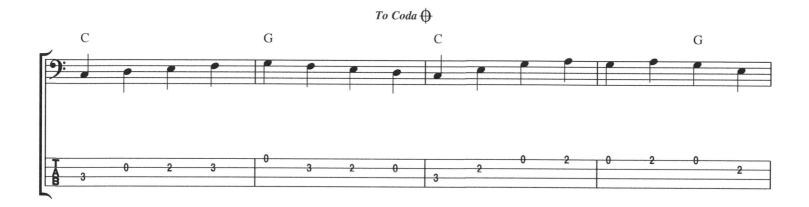

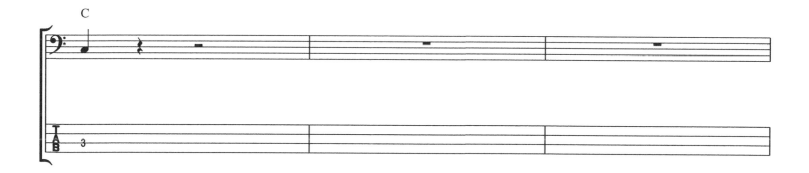

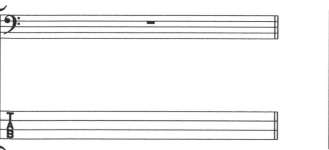

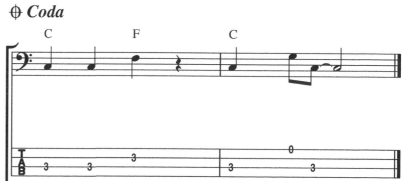

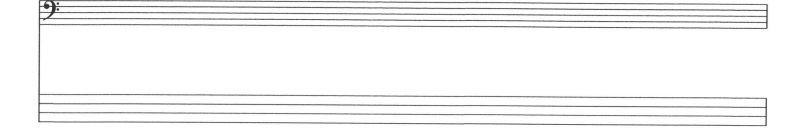

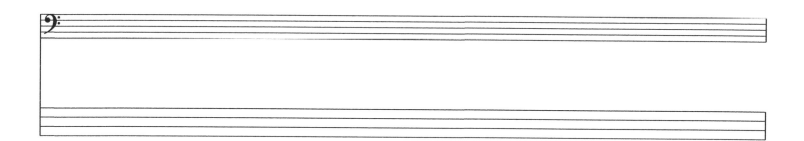

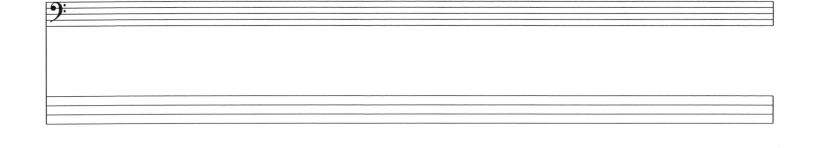

FastTrack is the fastest way for beginners to learn to play the instrument they just bought. **FastTrack** is different from other method books: we've made our book/audio packs user-friendly with plenty of cool songs that make it easy and fun for players to teach themselves. Plus, the last section of the books have the same songs so that students can form a band and jam together. Songbooks for guitar, bass, keyboard and drums are all compatible, and feature eight songs. All packs include great play-along audio with a professional-sounding back-up band.

FastTrack Bass
by Blake Neely & Jeff Schroedl

Level 1
00264732	Method Book/Online Media	$14.99
00697284	Method Book/Online Audio	$7.99
00696404	Method Book/Online Audio + DVD	$14.99
00697289	Songbook 1/Online Audio	$12.99
00695368	Songbook 2/Online Audio	$12.99
00696440	Rock Songbook with CD	$12.99
00696058	DVD	$7.99

Level 2
00697294	Method Book/Online Audio	$9.99
00697298	Songbook 1/Online Audio	$12.99
00695369	Songbook 2/Online Audio	$12.99

FastTrack Drum
by Blake Neely & Rick Mattingly

Level 1
00264733	Method Book/Online Media	$14.99
00697285	Method Book/Online Audio	$7.99
00696405	Method Book/Online Audio + DVD	$14.99
00697290	Songbook 1/Online Audio	$12.99
00695367	Songbook 2/Online Audio	$12.99
00696441	Rock Songbook with CD	$12.99
00696059	DVD	$7.99

Level 2
00697295	Method Book/Online Audio	$9.99
00697299	Songbook 1/Online Audio	$12.99
00695371	Songbook 2/Online Audio	$12.99

FastTrack Guitar
For Electric or Acoustic Guitar, or Both
by Blake Neely & Jeff Schroedl

Level 1
00264731	Method Book/Online Media	$14.99
00697282	Method Book/Online Audio	$7.99
00696403	Method Book/Online Audio + DVD	$14.99
00697287	Songbook 1/Online Audio	$12.99
00695343	Songbook 2/Online Audio	$12.99
00696438	Rock Songbook with CD	$12.99
00696057	DVD	$7.99

Level 2
00697286	Method Book/Online Audio	$9.99
00697296	Songbook/Online Audio	$14.99

Chords & Scales
00697291	Book/Online Audio	$10.99

FastTrack Keyboard
For Electric Keyboard, Synthesizer or Piano
by Blake Neely & Gary Meisner

Level 1
00264734	Method Book/Online Media	$14.99
00697283	Method Book/Online Audio	$7.99
00696406	Method Book/Online Audio + DVD	$14.99
00697288	Songbook 1/Online Audio	$12.99
00696439	Rock Songbook with CD	$12.99
00696060	DVD	$7.99

Level 2
00697293	Method Book/Online Audio	$9.99

Chords & Scales
00697292	Book/Online Audio	$9.99

FastTrack Harmonica
by Blake Neely & Doug Downing

Level 1
00695407	Method Book/Online Audio	$7.99
00695958	Mini Method Book with CD	$7.95
00820016	Mini Method/CD + Harmonica	$12.99
00695574	Songbook/Online Audio	$12.99

Level 2
00695889	Method Book/Online Audio	$9.99
00695891	Songbook with CD	$12.99

FastTrack Lead Singer
by Blake Neely

Level 1
00695408	Method Book/Online Audio	$7.99
00695410	Songbook/Online Audio	$14.99

Level 2
00695890	Method Book/Online Audio	$9.95
00695892	Songbook with CD	$12.95

FastTrack Saxophone
by Blake Neely

Level 1
00695241	Method Book/Online Audio	$7.99
00695409	Songbook/Online Audio	$14.99

FastTrack Ukulele
by Chad Johnson

Level 1
00114417	Method Book/Online Audio	$7.99
00158671	Songbook/Online Audio	$12.99

Level 2
00275508	Method Book/Online Audio	$9.99

FastTrack Violin
by Patrick Clark

Level 1
00141262	Method Book/Online Audio	$7.99

Visit Hal Leonard online at **www.halleonard.com**

Prices, contents, and availability subject to change without notice.
Some products may not be available outside the U.S.A. Spanish and French editions also available.

0920
021